# 7 Minutes!*

### * Average length of today's doctor visit

## How to Get the Most from *Your* Doctor Visit

### Marisa C. Weiss, M.D.

President and Founder, breastcancer.org

Photographs by Elias I. Friedman

RANDOM HOUSE
CUSTOM MEDIA

I would like to give a big thanks to my family, David, Elias, Henry, and Isabel, and a special thanks to my partners and friends, Richard Yelovich, M.D. (star of the book); Robin Cohen, R.N.; Al Denittis, M.D.; Hope Wohl; and my wonderful team of colleagues at breastcancer.org and Lankenau Hospital.

This book has been made possible, in part, by the 2006 Claneil Award.

To learn more about Random House Custom Media's branded content products, write to custommedia@randomhouse.com

ISBN 978-0-307-38350-1

Book design by Filip Zawodnik

Cover photography by Steve Belkowitz

Printed in the United States of America

First Edition

10 9 8 7 6 5 4 3 2 1

This book is dedicated to my wonderful friend and courageous patient Kelly Rooney, who inspired me to write this book. Kelly's strong compassion and fierce championship for all other people fighting for their precious lives can be felt in every word—and her boldness, originality, beauty, freshness, and vitality are peppered throughout each page. With this book, and in so many other ways, Kelly's legacy lives on through the generosity of The Kelly Rooney Foundation to provide continued comfort, support, joy, and inspiration.

THE
KELLY ROONEY
FOUNDATION

# Contents

# Introduction

My earliest memories of being a patient greatly influenced my decision to become a doctor. There was the unbearable embarrassment of being a six-year-old clutching the back of the blue gown to hold it shut and keep my naked tushy from hanging out. I sat for more than an hour in a Johns Hopkins waiting room (I was still wetting my bed and my parents wanted to know why). Years later, more embarrassment came in the form of a cold speculum and the equally cold response, "You better be!" at my first gynecologist appointment, after I told the doctor that I was still a virgin. There were special moments too. Twelve years later, the tear of compassion my obstetrician let loose when I appeared in the ER with my third miscarriage gave me hope and profound comfort at a time of loss.

Now, three healthy kids later, with twenty years of medical practice under my belt (or in the pocket of my white coat), I'm ready to bare all in order to make a real and healthy difference in the lives of women and men worldwide. Most patients need a crash training course to improve their relationships with their doctors so that they can get the best care possible.

How did I get here, a doctor offering advice about how to get the most out of your doctor visit? Ten years ago, I was asked to fill in a fifteen-minute gap in an all-day conference. What emerged was a practical but humorous presentation called "Doctor, Doctor, Lend Me Your Ear." I focused on the day we all love to hate—the day we have to go the doctor—from the perspectives of both patient and physician.

To my surprise, it was given the highest evaluation scores of any of the presentations at the conference. From there, the presentation turned into a live stand-up performance for audiences of both doctors and patients. Later, it was expanded to include other members of the health care team, such as nurses, pharmacists, medical students, and residents, as well as healthy people seeking routine care for themselves or their loved ones.

From coast to coast in the United States and also in Europe, this presentation has developed a cultlike following. Year after year, I've been asked to give repeat performances by prestigious medical centers such as Johns Hopkins, Memorial Sloan-Kettering, and the Cleveland Clinic and at lay health conferences, including Speaking of Women's Health. It's also been featured on DVD and television. For more than a decade, conference organizers and participants and media experts have said, "You have to turn this into a book!"

What finally pushed me into action was seeing my patients' vulnerability in the chaos of today's health care crisis. There are so many great new medical advances that could save lives. At the same time, patients have less time than ever—a mere seven minutes, on average—with their doctors to find out about them. How can you make the most out of those seven minutes to ensure that you take care of the one and only you? This book helps you work with your doctor to protect and cherish your precious life.

# ONE

## Scared and Sacred

The Relationship We Love
(and Sometimes Dread)

One of the most sacred bonds between two people is that of physician and patient. We've all heard the old adage "You have nothing if you don't have your health," and it's absolutely true. Your partnership with your doctor is designed to maintain and protect your health and well-being. You turn to a doctor when everything is going fine—such as when you're visiting for a routine checkup—and when everything isn't going fine, such as when you receive the diagnosis of disease. Fair weather or foul, your doctor is there for you, because of you, with you. For both the doctor and the patient, the relationship is vital. After all, without patients, the doctor would not exist.

Still, how many patients really get what we need from that relationship? How many of us know how to walk into that examination room feeling confident, well-prepared, and in control? Too few, in my experience. So I've decided to jump in to help improve the situation.

**Me—the doctor. In charge, in uniform . . . in a hurry?**

*Wait a minute*, you might be thinking. *The last thing I need is another lecture from Dr. Big Shot M.D.* When you picked up this book, perhaps you expected me to talk about the doctor-patient relationship from the perspective of the doctor—since most of my adult life is spent being a doctor. The reality is, however, that I've been a patient a lot longer than I've been a doctor.

So, if you prefer, you can find a few books on the shelf in which a doctor will lecture you in the dry, complicated vernacular of medicine about what you should be doing at the doctor visit. But I think it might be a little bit more interesting, and a little more helpful to you, if I do this from the perspective of the experienced patient that I am.

*Bear with me. This will only take a minute.*

**OK, I guess it's my turn now. Strip down, gown on—open in the back.**

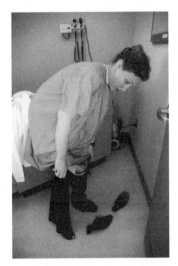

Hmmm . . . forgot these socks had holes in them!

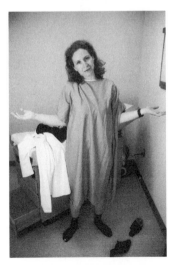

And they call this a gown?!

When would you ever choose to wear something like this to an important meeting about your future? I'm sure I'm not the only one who feels diminished, inadequate, nearly naked, and cold in this outfit that they call a "gown." For most big meetings, you would wear a power suit or at least something neat and professional. When you're at your place of business, your clothes cover most of your body, things sort of match, and your underwear isn't hanging out. You feel empowered and ready for work.

There are a number of things that you can do as a patient to get the best care possible. I'll show you how to retain your sense of power, even in that most vulnerable of situations: the oh-so-scary but oh-so-sacred doctor visit.

## Patient, Client, or Consumer?

In this book, I use the most common traditional term, "patient." According to *The American Heritage Dictionary,* the word "patient" is a noun that means a sick, injured, wounded, or other person requiring medical care or treatment. But the definition of the adjective "patient"—one who is able to put up with pain, trouble, delay, or boredom, without complaining—can heavily color the experience of being a patient.

Some doctors now use the term "client" or "consumer" to emphasize the fact that patients choose doctors for specific services. These new ways of referring to patients attempt to shift the power dynamic between the doctor and the people he or she treats. Still, these terms leave something to be desired, putting an undue emphasis on the business aspect of the relationship. They underplay the nurturing that we hope to receive from doctors. Ultimately, using the word "client" is supposed to level the playing field, but the fact is that it is still an inherently lopsided relationship.

# TWO

## 7 Minutes

So Much to Say, So Little Time

**M**odern medicine has brought us so many new advances in the diagnosis and treatment of all kinds of health challenges—from allergies, infection, and joint deterioration to heart disease, diabetes, and cancer. With little time to find out about these medical breakthroughs from their doctors, patients can be at a disadvantage. Some studies show that the average amount of time per appointment that a doctor spends with a patient is seven minutes. Seven minutes for one of the most essential meetings in your life!

Of course we know that many doctors usually spend much more than seven minutes behind the scenes, before, during, and after your visit, as they read up on your medical situation, review your diagnostic studies, evaluate prior and ongoing therapies, and connect with the other doctors and nurses on your team. Plus, it's certainly true that many patients get much more than seven minutes with their doctors, depending on what they need and on the nature of the appointment. You may have many medical needs requiring a long visit or just a few fleeting concerns that could easily be resolved in five minutes.

The burden of making treatment decisions can feel so heavy on your shoulders, especially when you feel rushed and so much is at stake. Making sense of all the complex medical information being thrown at you can make you feel overwhelmed, confused, and pressured. You may be up against some pretty big decisions in a short period of time, and sometimes your life is literally on the line.

There's nothing like illness, or even the most benign visit to the doctor's office, to remind you that your life is a gift. You deserve the best care possible, but taking care of yourself is a big responsibility. I'm here to tell you that you can do it, but you don't have to do it alone. With a lot of essential collaboration from your doctor, you can effectively take care of your precious life.

For the past twenty years, I've been a physician who takes care of women with breast cancer. Despite this fact, when I'm in the role of patient, my whole experience—whether at the hospital, the clinic, the doctor's office, or consulting with health care practitioners by phone—is always from the perspective of the mother of three teenage children.

*They are Elias, Isabel, and Henry.*

**Who would make sure they're safe if not me?**

In my role as Mom, my first worry is what will happen to my children if anything happens to me. Even though my kids are well past infancy, they need me to guide them, to love them, and to make sure they return home safely. I have to guard and cherish my health for *their* sake as well as mine.

# THREE

## Your Medical Team

The Doctor-Patient Relationship

Over the years, I have had many different doctors on my team, and you probably do, too. Your team may include a primary care doctor, a gynecologist, a surgeon, a radiologist, a dentist, an allergist, a fertility expert, and/or an oncologist. The list may be even longer than that, depending on your health concerns. So many doctors can make a person feel sick! But if you have a significant medical concern or condition, the reality is that one doctor can't manage or treat you as effectively as a team of specialized physicians can. Ensuring that you get the best possible care means getting the best doctor from each specialty working in tandem with your primary care physician. When you have so many doctors on your team, sometimes you might wonder: Who's in charge? Who is going to coordinate all the various doctors and different tests and treatments? Am I my own head honcho?

You might think that's a scary thought, but it's really the best possible news. It means that you're in charge of choosing the best care within each specialty. You're the point person who, with your doctors' support, ensures that your care is coordinated among all the various physicians in different specialties.

To do that effectively, you need to be sure that you give each doctor your whole medical picture. Provide each with up-to-date medical records and contact information for all of your other doctors to facilitate communication. This can also prevent unnecessary or duplicate tests or treatments, and ensure that you are getting the care that you need—without anything falling between the cracks.

**My medical team. Why do they look so worried?
Is there something they're not telling me?**

## One-to-One

The doctor-patient relationship is so important, intense, private, and intimate. But it's also inherently very lopsided, and using the term "client" instead of "patient" doesn't change this reality. I'm not being critical here—it's just the way this relationship is. Think about some of the reasons for this:

- **You're the one with a health concern, while your doctor is presumably well.**

- **You're wearing a patient gown, cold and nearly naked, while your doctor is dressed, warm, and looks quite distinguished.**

- **You're unfamiliar with medical terminology, while your doctor is fluent in this foreign-to-you language.**

- **You're referring to your physician as Dr. So-and-So, while he or she might take the liberty of calling you by your first name.**

- **You're playing on the doctor's turf, with his or her schedule and team, while your schedule is secondary.**

- **You're paying a lot of money to see this medical team, whereas the value of your time may be overlooked.**

This power imbalance begins before you even get to the office. Think about all the things that you need to do just to get to the doctor's office on time. You rearrange your life—your job, where your boss thinks of a sick day as a sign of weakness; your kids, who have band practice, soccer, karate, and other activities; your dog, who chews table legs if left alone in the house all day; the carpet cleaner, who arrived two days earlier than scheduled. Well, you get my point. It's not easy to find the time, but we all have to do it.

And I have to do it, too. Doctors don't get out of this universal challenge. We have to wear the gown just like everyone else. How about you come with me as I go to the doctor? Then you can see just what I mean.

# FOUR

## Do I Look Fat in Red?

Getting Ready for the Doctor Visit

**B**efore you follow me to my doctor visit, there is one thing you need to know: I worry. I think of all the things that the doctor might tell me—none of them good news. The night before is usually a sleepless one. That is usually when I see my husband the most—sleeping.

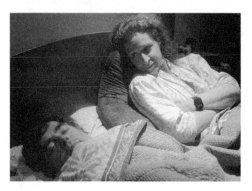

**Watching David sleep.**

The white ceiling of our bedroom becomes the screen for that night's horror flicks. Without the usual distractions running through the day, there's just me and my fears featured in 3-D IMAX fashion.

To help you get a good night's sleep, take some time during the day to prepare a list of questions that you want to ask your doctor. Getting your concerns down on paper can help ease the worry that you will leave your appointment without the answers that you need. Think of it as an equation: less worry plus better preparation equals more sleep.

## Symptom Reporting Sheet

Take a few moments to think through these questions about any symptoms that you have and jot down the answers. These are common questions that many doctors will ask, and preparation will help you save precious time during your appointment.

1. What is your symptom?

2. What does it feel like? (For example: Is the pain sharp, dull, burning, aching, throbbing?)

3. Where is the symptom or pain located? Does it move to another area?

4. When did it start?

5. What were you doing when it first started?

6. Have you ever had it before?

7. How is your current symptom similar to or different from last time?

8. How long does it last?

9. Is the symptom getting better? Worse? Or staying the same?

10. What makes it better?

11. What makes it go away?

12. Does it happen at any particular time of day or night?

13. Are there other signs or symptoms that go along with it?

14. Does anyone else in your family or circle of friends also have a similar symptom?

15. What medications are you taking? Are there any new ones?

16. Have you used any new products? Done anything different recently?

After you have made a list of your symptoms, take some time to review them and think of the questions you want to ask during the appointment. Stage your own informal rehearsal. First, find a quiet spot with two chairs. Sit in one of them, and imagine your thoughts and feelings sitting on the other. As you ask yourself some key questions, listen to your answers with your mind, heart, and soul. You'll see that new feelings and insights will come out. Write down what emerges; sort things out then or later. Put the questions and concerns in order of priority. There—you've done a lot of the hard stuff before you even got in to the doctor's office. You're ready and you're in sync with yourself. That's taking care of yourself; you've just made yourself feel better. Good!

In order to arrive fully prepared for your visit, make sure you have the following assembled in your purse the night before—if your mornings are like mine, the time before you leave will evaporate so quickly there will be no margin to search for a missing insurance card or checkbook.

## Office Visit Checklist

There are a number of things you might need when you visit the doctor's office:

- **Health insurance card**
- **Photo identification**
- **Social security number**
- **Credit card and checkbook for office visit fee or co-pay**
- **Completed forms that the doctor's office might have sent you ahead of time**
- **Copies of any relevant medical records, test results, or radiology examinations, such as a chest X-ray, CT scan, etc., that the doctor might need**
- **Pathology slides, if they're from an outside hospital—doctors usually want their own pathologists to verify the outside pathology interpretations**
- **Your list of questions**
- **Pen and paper for taking notes**
- **Any referrals required by your insurance company**

If you are seeing a doctor in the same hospital where all of your tests were done, you usually don't have to bring your films.

As night lightens to dawn, I finally fall asleep. The sound of the alarm is terribly unwelcome to me, but my husband seems to leap out of bed, carefree and ready for the new day. Even the morning newscasters are more chipper than usual. Meanwhile, all I want to do is hide under the covers and fall back to sleep. Instead, I have to rip myself out of bed and begin the ritual of getting ready for the doctor visit.

On the morning of the medical appointment, your normal routine might go out the window as you prepare for any situation at the doctor's office, including getting naked in front of a stranger. Be sure to allow yourself some extra time so that you're not frantically racing around the house trying to get there on time.

If you're like me, you worry about what you should do to get ready. The first task for me is shaving those legs. I always remember to perform this ritual—ever since the time that I *thought* I had shaved my legs before rushing to the doctor's office. I made my way into the examination room and got undressed. Then, I looked down. Whoa! There I was: half man, half woman. I had shaved one leg but not the other.

There are other concerns, too. For example, if you're a woman visiting your gynecologist, what should you do if you discover you'll have your period just before the appointment? Should you change your appointment? Should you douche—that *thing* that some women do? Many women choose to skip their doctor visit

**Should have started yesterday. I am going to need
the lawn mower and the Weedwacker.**

if they have their period. Getting a reliable Pap test and doing a breast exam is easier when you're not menstruating. Still, it's best not to assume; instead, discuss the situation with your doctor. If you believe that the timing is bad, call your doctor's office just to make sure. Keep your appointment if it's not an issue. Reschedule if your doctor thinks a later time would be better.

The panic that you're feeling may make you rethink keeping your appointment. Or you may have other reasons why you need to cancel. While you might find many excuses to miss your appointment, there is no excuse for not calling to cancel. Be courteous to your doctor by making your cancellation twenty-four hours in advance so that the valuable time slot can be filled by another patient. A no-show without a cancellation call is not a good way to build a good relationship with your doctor.

## Reasons Why People Cancel Doctor's Appointments at the Last Minute

- **Illness**
- **Menstrual period**
- **Unexpected event or family emergency**
- **More pressing medical issues being handled by another doctor**
- **Hospitalization**
- **The fee is too expensive**
- **Forgetting the appointment**
- **Weather—either too bad to travel or too nice to stay indoors at the doctor's office**
- **Vacation**
- **Feel better and decide not to go to the doctor**
- **Avoidance**

You're still going? Great. Now it's time to get dressed. But what do you wear? Is it time for the leopard-print blouse? Should you wear a suit? Or are comfy yoga pants a better option? What goes under: a thong or a matronly white brief? Or does it even matter because by the time the doctor sees you, you're already in the hospital gown?

I always dress as if I'm going to a high-level business meeting. It helps me feel empowered and strong. You should choose clothes

**Too big. Too dowdy. No, not that one, either.**

that make you feel good about yourself. I saw this in a new way once when I was preparing for a doctor visit and my mother said to me, "Marisa, what do you care about what you wear—you're young, slender, and attractive. Anyone would want to take care of you. But look at me, I'm just a lumpy old bag—who would want to even bother?!"

Appalled, I replied, "Mom . . . wow . . . this is an important relationship between you and your doctor. If you present yourself in a way that makes you feel unworthy and not entitled to your doctor's time, your doctor is going to pick up those cues."

Giving off such cues could be dangerous. The doctor might spend less time with you if he or she senses that you aren't serious about your own health care. You might have fewer questions answered.

My mother took my advice to heart and has since started wearing smart-looking outfits and big necklaces to her visits. Even if the doctor doesn't notice, it gives her that extra bit of confidence she needs to feel powerful.

Please, don't think you're unworthy of your doctor's interest—as my mother once did. Whether you are a size 6, 16, or larger, whether you are bald from chemo or have a great head of hair, you're the star of this show. Get ready for that appointment the way you would for any important occasion in your life. It's all about you—you and your health. Hop on that examination table like the royalty that you are.

## Bring Your Own Gown

There are many reasons you may want to bring your own gown to your next doctor's appointment:

- **The gown will fit you properly. Standard-issue gowns are too small for many people.**

- **Your own gown may keep you warmer.**

- **You may feel more confident and presentable.**

- **A simple lightweight bathrobe will do—terry cloth is too thick. Just make sure your gown has a full opening in the front or back so that you can be properly examined.**

Even though I'm dressed, I'm still not ready. It takes far more than a great outfit to get out the door. For me, there are three obstacles: Henry, Isabel, and Elias. I've got to get my kids out of bed and make sure they get to school or work before I'm free to head to the doctor.

Finally, the kids are out the door, and now it's time to race around and fight traffic to get to the doctor's office on time. You might find it helpful to plot the route in advance, allowing extra time in case you encounter traffic or other unexpected delays. Knowing approximately how much time you need to ensure that you arrive on time can alleviate anxiety. With good planning, instead of arriving an hour early or an hour late, you can get there with plenty of time to worry about other things.

# FIVE

## On Time!

Arriving at the Doctor's Office

It's a miracle. You made it on time, and in one piece. There were no accidents, and you're still presentable. Getting there is only the first hurdle. Next, you try to get the attention of the many office staff members who appear to be totally caught up in some big juicy story. Did one just get engaged? See a great movie last night?

*You feel invisible.*

**Yoo-hoo! Helloooo!**

Finally, after you clear your throat a few times, someone turns around and welcomes you. You may get a nice warm welcome that quickly makes you feel much better and confident and sure that you're in the right place.

*Sometimes, however, you can't help but notice that the sight of you might have made the smile drop off her face.*

**Maybe she had a bad morning . . . or does she already dislike me? What did I do to make her feel that way?**

What do you do? Take a deep breath. Remind yourself that you're there on a very important mission—caring for your health. Take the high road. If the receptionist is cranky, it's not your fault and it's best not to let that bother you. It's too early in the process to use up your precious personal energy. You can say, "I'm so glad to be here, because I really appreciate the chance to see the doctor. I'm sorry to have to interrupt your conversation." Get her name and thank her for her help (even if she wasn't very helpful).

Next you register, fill out a bunch of other extra forms, and hand over any medical records and X-ray films. Just remember to collect your outside films when the visit is over.

*Then, it's time to wait.*

**Finally. A chance to read the entire magazine.**

At first, the wait can be relaxing. There aren't any children demanding your attention, and there's no laundry to be done or boss putting extra stacks of work on your desk. And you're exactly where you need to be.

*But then the wait drags on. You wait.*
*Then you wait some more.*

**Cut my hair? Leave it long? Flared pants or skinny?**
**I refuse to read this fashion insert one more time.**

You think to yourself, *Where is the doctor? Is he playing poker or something? What's next? A call to his stockbroker?*

**I don't know about him, but I'm folding.**

*And then you wait some more.*

By this time, the waiting game has gotten really old. You've read all of last month's magazine and even the ancient stack of *National Geographic* issues in the waiting room. You may have seen other people who arrived after you taken back to see the doctor before you. Were they given the same appointment time? Did you arrive early and they came late? Is their "case" more urgent than yours—or is that person rich or famous? You have too much time to wonder why. Of course it's much more likely that your doctor has had a string of patients with complex medical issues requiring extra-long discussions, unscheduled phone calls from other doctors, interruptions to share just-released test results with patients, and so on. Doctors' days are predictably unpredictable; the schedule often gets backed up and it's usually dark when they go home. As much as you might understand this as a patient, it may still be hard to handle because by this point you might be worn down by hunger, frustration, uncertainty, and fatigue.

**If only I had a sleeping bag, I'd crawl right in.**

Eventually the receptionist comes to get you. But why does she need to BLAST your name out over the whole waiting room?!

*"M-A-R-I-S-A W-E-I-S-S! IS THERE A MER-IT-ZA WISE
HERE—ANYWHERE?!" Say good-bye to privacy!*

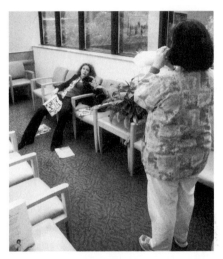

**I was having a nice dream. . . .**

I remember a time when my family members and I were wait-ing in a genetics testing center for the results of the test for the breast cancer gene. We scurried in and found a corner in the back of the waiting room, as well as some big newspapers behind which we could hide. We wanted to escape the view of several people in the room whom we recognized.

The newspaper wall was working just fine until my name was broadcast over the loudspeaker. I was being called back to see the doctor, but it felt as if I was starring in a public awareness campaign aired to the entire population of the waiting room. I was embarrassed and upset by the loss of privacy just when my family and I needed it the most.

## Things to Bring to the Waiting Room

- **Cell phone and charger**
- **Call list**
- **Printed schedule for the rest of the day with contact numbers in case of delays**
- **Paper (blank notebook is best) and pens that work**
- **Book**
- **Magazines**
- **Post-it notes**
- **Things to do with your hands: knitting, writing, list-making, crossword puzzles, balancing your checkbook, etc.**
- **Something to eat and drink**

# SIX

## Absolutely Indispensable

The Nurse

The long wait seems to be over, but you feel as if you made a reservation at a fancy restaurant months ago but still had to wait nearly an hour. You stand up with a mixture of relief, irritation, and urgency as you grab your stuff. Finally, you're about to see the nurse and then the doctor. You're led into the examination room and there's the nurse. She seems like someone you could truly like and who really cares about you.

This is a good time to let her know what's on your mind so that she can note it in your chart and brief the doctor. Be sure to provide updates on medical and other significant events. Are you stressed out over your children's school situation? Did your partner just lose his or her job? Was a relative just diagnosed with cancer? Are you looking for the name of a new gynecologist? Is there a test result you are seeking? By providing answers to these questions, you can more quickly resolve uncertainty, minimize anxiety, and clarify the issues you want to discuss with the doctor.

**She's so warm and helpful. Do I still need to see the doctor?**

Once, in my role as a doctor, during a routine visit with a woman I had taken care of for many years, I was trying to explain something, but she seemed so distracted.

"Mary, I feel like we're not connecting today. You seem preoccupied with something. What's on your mind?" I asked.

"What about that bone scan?" she asked.

"Bone scan? What bone scan?" I replied.

"The bone scan," she repeated, "I saw Dr. Cohen last week. He ordered a bone scan. Do you have the results?"

Clearly, this is what had been weighing on her mind. If she had told my nurse up front, we would have been able to immediately get to work on tracking down the results, so that we could move on to other topics. As it happened, we were able to get the results, which were clear. However, we did lose precious appointment time because I didn't know about the situation ahead of time. As a patient, I also find it hard to ask difficult questions. Still, I know I have to ask them or else I won't get what I need from the visit.

*Once you've unloaded your questions and concerns,*
*it's time to approach the dreaded scale.*

**Uh-oh. I have a wedgie or something's hanging out!**

Suddenly, a feeling of guilt washes over you as you think about last night when you wolfed down most of that chocolate cake.

# SEVEN

## (Do the) Limbo

After the Nurse, Before the Doctor

As soon as the nurse leaves the **examination room, and before the doctor comes in, it's time for me to head for the paper towel rack.** I don't know about you, but I sweat when I'm nervous. Got to get rid of any extra moisture before I get examined! I move quickly because, of course, the threat of the doctor walking in and catching me in the act only makes the sweating worse!

Once I'm dry again, it's time to sit down and wait some more.

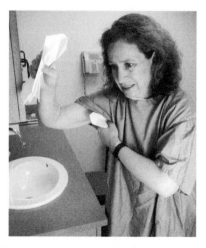

**Why just armpits? I need body antiperspirant!**

We've all had to spend some time in the examination room, waiting for the doctor. You might be reading yet another vintage copy of *People* magazine. Then, you see it sitting there, just a foot away—your medical chart. That manila folder stuffed with your medical history and all of your doctor's cryptic notes about you. In fact, the chart may have that test result that you're seeking, or secret information about you. What could be a more fascinating read?

*So, you sneak a peek. But then the doctor walks in.*

**What does "asymmetric fibrous stroma" mean, anyway?**

And you feel a little awkward and embarrassed, kind of like he caught you reading a letter sent home for your parents.

**Caught you!**

Don't worry. This is your medical chart, and you do have the right to read it. While the physical or electronic chart itself belongs in the doctor's office as his or her permanent record, you're entitled to receive copies of everything in it. In fact, it's a good idea to ask the doctor's secretary or office manager for copies of your medical records along the way, including radiology and laboratory test reports, operative notes, pathology reports, and consultation letters. That way, you can easily keep an up-to-date file of your own in case another doctor needs it.

If your chart is part of an electronic record system, then you may be able to access it yourself on the computer with special passwords.

You're also in charge of who sees your medical records. In order to disclose them to others, the doctor needs written permission that is signed and dated, along with specific doctors' names and addresses in order to release them to those parties. Some centers even require a signed permission form for them to release records to you. That goes for family and friends, too—even your nearest and dearest don't have the right to see your medical records unless you've given them permission. The HIPAA website (www.hhs.gov/ocr/hipaa) will give you detailed rules.

If you need copies of your chart, you should check to see what your doctor's office policy is. While most doctors' offices and medical centers will copy a few pages and send them to a few places at no charge, copying large files might involve a fee for copying, as well as postage or courier fees, particularly if the records need to be sent overnight. Some offices require a few days' lead time or will only copy records on particular days of the week, when they are adequately staffed.

Providing the office with addressed and stamped envelopes (make sure there's enough postage) makes the process go faster and more smoothly.

If your medical chart is electronic, you might be given a compact disc (CD) or a link to a password-protected website that houses the records. You are then free to pass along the CD, make another copy of it, or print out the relevant pages yourself.

To keep your file organized, use a three-ring binder and tabs so you can find the records quickly. Bring this with you whenever you visit the doctor. It's not uncommon for your doctor to need a copy of a record. If he or she needs it, and you have it, that's great partnership at work. Having your own copy of your medical records allows you to check for accuracy. You can ensure that the file refers to the right "Mary Jones" and that the lump is correctly noted as being in the right breast, instead of the left. You can double-check notes about family history, medications, and information from other doctors to ensure that they are accurate.

# EIGHT

## The Doctor Cometh

First Impressions

f you're visiting a new practice or there's a new doctor on the team, you might have no idea what to expect when that door opens. The doctor might not look any older than your own children! How can such a young doctor have the experience that you really need?

Before you lose confidence, find out more. Keep in mind that doctors often do look younger than their age because they are usually working inside all the time with very little sun exposure.

**She's even too young to drive.**
**Did she have to catch a school bus to get to work?**

It's okay to express your concern with a compliment rolled in. You might say something like, "Wow, you've accomplished so much so early in your young life! That's just terrific, but I do need to feel reassured that you have the level of experience that I believe I need. Can you tell me about your training and experience?" Usually, young doctors are used to reassuring people about their level of expertise. If, after you have given the doctor a chance to respond, you're not satisfied, you can give the doctor another chance, or you can find another doctor. You have the power to improve the situation if it's not working for you.

Sometimes when that door opens up, a whole army comes charging in.

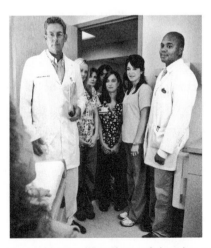

**Whoa, what a big team. What if one of them has to go to the bathroom . . . do the rest of them wait outside the door?**

Who are all these people?! Can they even fit in the room? You are way outnumbered! This kind of situation can make most patients shrink, feeling *even more* overwhelmed, embarrassed, guinea pig–like—lost with no privacy. This team-based approach is common, especially in teaching hospitals, where there are doctors at various levels of their training.

---

## Medical Team Members at a Teaching Hospital

There are many different doctors in a teaching hospital, each at various stages of their careers.

**Attending:** The main doctor in charge, also the one whom you were probably scheduled to see. It could be your internist, gynecologist, or surgeon, or a specialist like a cardiologist, an infectious disease doctor, or an oncologist.

**Fellow:** A doctor who has finished his or her residency and is getting further specialty training. For example, a general surgeon may go on to a plastic surgery fellowship, or a medical doctor may become a fellow in heart, lung, or cancer care. A fellow is also being groomed to become an attending within a few years.

---

**Chief resident:** A doctor at the end of his or her general residency program who is selected to serve as a leader among resident peers. A chief resident may also go on for extra training in order to become a specialist.

**Resident:** A doctor undergoing training in the core of his or her area of medicine. This can mean general surgery, medicine, radiology, etc. A resident may go on for extra training in order to become a specialist.

**Intern:** A doctor fresh out of medical school, just starting to get hands-on experience and responsibility for patient care. Most of what he or she does is keep track of each patient's day-to-day inpatient care. Working with the rest of the medical team, an intern may follow vital signs, fluid balances, and test results, as well as coordinate treatment plans.

**Medical student:** This doctor-in-training might be at any level of his or her four years of medical school. The medical student works together with the team and helps with all kinds of tasks, such as taking medical histories and performing physical exams, drawing blood, coordinating information, etc., depending on level of training.

NOTE: There can be several people in the roles of resident, intern, and medical student.

While it can be gratifying to have so many people involved in your care, it can also be overwhelming. Plus, if you're experiencing an embarrassing medical problem, such as low libido, hair loss, vaginal itch and discharge, toenail fungus, crying spells at work, or big weight gain despite best intentions, you may not be ready to announce these sensitive personal issues to a large audience. They deserve careful attention during a one-on-one meeting with your doctor.

If you're dealing with a sensitive issue, it's OK for you to say to the head doctor, "I've had a hard time lately and I really don't feel comfortable with an audience. Is it okay for me to meet with just you today?" That is a very reasonable request.

Then again, many of you might feel at ease having all these people squeeze into your examination room. If you regularly visit a teaching hospital or an associated medical center, you may have come to expect this. You may even feel reassured by having more people accountable for your care. If you are comfortable with the big medical team approach, the doctor in charge should be prepared to introduce you to at least the key members on his or her team. (A lengthy introduction of the whole army might consume your whole seven minutes!)

Now, if you don't mind the big team but you are still feeling vulnerable and diminished, you can bring your own team of people with you.

**OK, folks, smile and look friendly. Don't bite the doctor!**

Building up *your own* side of the ratio is a great solution. But before you enlist your personal cheering squad, keep a few things in mind. Be sure to introduce these people to your doctor, and let your doctor know what kind of information can be revealed in front of them. Otherwise your doctor might say too little, out of respect for your privacy. Or, if the doctor is rushed and not mindful of your privacy, he or she might spill some beans that you'd prefer to keep in the can.

When the medical team looms large, or when *your* entourage is big, break up the visit into two parts. You can include the whole team for the first part, but then limit the rest of the visit to just the main doctor and, perhaps, your closest family member or friend. The physical exam is the perfect time to make this shift. Use this opportunity to share the sensitive personal stuff that you want to keep private. As you leave for the examination room, thank the rest of your group for their support.

Whether it's a spouse, a trusted friend, or an entire entourage, bringing others with you has a number of benefits. Aside from moral support, you have another set of eyes and ears that can observe body language, as well as listen to what the doctor is saying. A third—or fourth or fifth—party can ask tough questions that you might not feel comfortable asking on your own. A spouse or a friend can jump in and continue the conversation if you're feeling overwhelmed and exhausted. Also, if you have a family member or a trusted friend who has specialized expertise—a nurse in the family, for example—that person can be a more informed interpreter for you, particularly when you're getting a full diagnosis or you're up against a big decision.

Let the doctor know what you want disclosed in front of your companions and what needs to stay off the record. Unless you specify otherwise, assume that the people you bring to the doctor's office will hear all the information that is revealed to you, including sensitive information.

If there is a long list of don't-talk-abouts, then maybe you would be better off doing the visit solo and only bringing your family or friends in at the end in a more controlled setting. Or you might limit your support team to only the person or people that you trust with private information. It is also possible to start your meeting with family and friends and then ask your doctor for a few minutes alone at the end. But be careful—this opportunity at the end may fly away if the doctor runs out of time.

If you're bringing others to your appointment, you need to prepare your family and friends. Give them each The Rules and specific job descriptions.

## Rules for Family and Friends

### DO

- Follow your job description: drive, handle the tape recorder, carry my stuff, and be responsible for food and drinks.

- Always let me talk first.

- Wait for your cue to ask your assigned question. (Agree on the cue before you go in—like a hand signal or a verbal introduction: "Dad, you were going to ask Dr. Jones more about . . . ")

- Ask permission before you jump in if you don't have a specific cue.

- Use my name when you talk about me in front of the doctor.

- Turn off your cell phone. (That goes for BlackBerries, iPods, and any other electronic devices. Just think of my appointment as you would a plane taking off.)

- Bring a notebook and pens—and a tape recorder if we agree upon this up front.

- Watch the doctor's body language.

- Come fed, freshly showered, and properly dressed—nice neat clothes, no stains.

- Be patient with me! I may be feeling more emotional than usual.

- Ask if you can join me during the physical exam.

## DON'T

- **Talk over me.**

- **Interrupt me.**

- **Wear perfume or cologne.**

- **Mention every doctor you know.**

- **Eat food, open candy, or slurp down drinks when the doctor is present.**

- **Come if you have to be somewhere else right afterward—in case my appointment is delayed and that puts you in a bind.**

- **Assume that you can represent me to my doctor on my behalf or request information about me in the future. Ask for my permission first.**

- **Demand to know details if they aren't any of your business.**

- **Be upset with my long list of rules. This is my health and I'm doing my best to protect it.**

After making The Rules clear, stop and thank your support team for helping you regain and fortify your health.

# NINE

## Advocating for
## a Family Member

Leaping over the Pitfalls

think about the hundreds of times you've been a patient. Now, add in those times when you have served as the health advocate for *another* patient, such as bringing your kids to checkups or driving elderly parents to appointments. Even spouses and friends sometimes need our hand or our voice when visiting the doctor.

Being a parent is great practice for speaking up for someone else. Once, I had to take my five-year-old son to the pediatrician for a high fever and an ear infection. The secretary managed to work us into the doctor's already overbooked schedule, for which we were very grateful. So, I was not too upset or angry about the hour-and-a-half wait in the waiting room. I could even understand the forty-five-minute wait in the examination room, even though my sick kid was shivering in a paper gown. But what came next sent my blood pressure through the roof.

The door to the examination room finally flung open and in marched a doctor who was not our regular doctor, whom we had been told to expect. Without so much as a "Hello, my name is Dr. So-and-So . . . ," the doctor buried his head in my son's chart as he muttered something about the fever. There was no eye contact. Who was this intruder? Stricken with stranger anxiety, my son flew into my lap for protection. Like water about to boil, my anger started to overwhelm me; I had to do something fast.

I jumped up, stuck out my hand, and leaned in with a big smile and said, "Hello, my name is Marisa Weiss and this is my son Elias. What is your name?"

The doctor stopped in his tracks, smiled at us, and introduced himself; my kid relaxed and I cooled off. We were back on track, ready for take two of the appointment. Disaster averted! Not only was it critical that I dealt with my anger, since it's difficult to relate very well to someone when furious, but I was also able to teach my son by example. Lesson learned: You need to make sure that your relationship with your doctor, or even a substitute doctor, is working for you. If you're not happy or comfortable, you can take measures to improve it.

What if it's your significant other or parent for whom you're advocating? This relationship can be quite a bit trickier. You can't control your partner's patient-doctor relationship, nor should you want to. Your spouse or parent is in charge of his or her own care and is entitled to the same privacy that you would expect for yourself (check out the HIPAA website, www.hhs.gov/ocr/hipaa). You want that person to stay in charge as long as possible. Your role is that of supporter, coach, or facilitator.

First, help your partner organize his or her questions and concerns, and prepare a report of any signs and symptoms prior to the doctor visit. To avoid a situation where your partner or parent withholds important information that his or her doctor may need to know, there are strings you *can* pull to make sure that things go as well as possible:

- **Mention to your partner or parent that this information should be included.**

- **Help prepare a to-discuss list and slip the missing information in there.**

- **Offer to go along to the visit.**

- **Push it to—and maybe over—the line and give the doctor a call ahead of time with the extra information.**

For example, let's say your husband's cholesterol and blood pressure are too high. You've done everything you can, including making sure that his dinner plate is loaded with organic vegetables, low-fat protein, and whole-wheat bread.

But then one day you catch him with fast food, blowing the whole nutritional plan.

In this kind of situation, you need to put one HIPAA in front of the other, and wiggle around some of the rules. You're allowed to disclose information to your family member's doctor, but HIPAA laws forbid the doctor from divulging information to you without your partner's permission.

Give the doctor a call to share the information if you are concerned that your family member is not going to be forthcoming. His or her doctor needs to know key information, such as the following:

1. Is he not taking his medicine?

2. Is he saying that he's exercising, and he really isn't?

3. Has your parent stopped eating, lost weight, or become forgetful, combative, or prone to bathroom accidents and falling spells?

4. Have your parents moved to an assisted-living facility?

5. Has one parent passed on and now the other is living alone?

If you answered yes to *any* of the above questions and you suspect that your spouse or family member won't share that information with his or her doctor, it's time to jump into that conversation. Your family member's doctor really needs to know these things, especially if it's been a dog's life since the doctor has actually seen him or her.

If your significant other is like mine, he refuses to go to his doctor, insisting that all is well unless he's had a hacking cough for six months or a fever in the triple digits.

Do you—like me—have to take special measures to get your spouse to the doctor?

**Try to escape and you'll end up in the slammer!**

There's a lot you can do to facilitate your family member's best care. Urge him or her to keep a medication list and make an allergy record, including medicines, contrast dye for tests, food, and other allergens. Make sure that he or she has contact information for all doctors and pharmacies and an up-to-date list of past medical and surgical events and procedures. The doctor needs to know about everything from heart attacks to blood pressure issues to appendix removal. And don't forget routine surveillance studies such as mammograms, stool checks for blood, bone density tests, colonoscopies, stress tests, eye checks, and so on.

Watching for oversights and mistakes will help avoid repeating tests unnecessarily if they were done recently but overlooked. Confirm with the doctor if the new medication is compatible with existing regular medications, and if your family member has any relevant allergies. If there is weight loss or gain, check if medication doses need to be recalculated. Make sure that the medical insurance bills have been paid or an alternative arrangement found.

No doubt, all of this can add up to a lot of work. Are you so saddled with the medical care of everyone else in your life that you are neglecting your own care? Do you feel like flushing your phone down the toilet and hiding?

Or do you feel like running away?

**Going to Alaska?**

We all know this kind of added stress is not good for our health, and it's only natural to want to escape. But there's an easy prescription to protect your own health and fight the blues: Take time for yourself. Instead of waiting for that big block of time off that never seems to come or that far-away vacation on the horizon, grab ten minutes a day *just* for you. Make it a priority. Indulge yourself. Plus, regular exercise is key. Do what brings you relief and comfort, and what makes you happy, because if you're dragging, you can't hold anyone up. Yoga can be remarkably restorative. I like to combine walking and retail therapy.

**I wonder what's on sale today?**

But watch out—this can get dangerous at the end of the month when the bill arrives.

# TEN

## Setting the Stage for Mutual Respect

Communicating with Your Doctor

**W**henever you start a serious meeting about your future, it's a good idea to greet the person with whom you're meeting. The exchange of eye contact forms a bond. It's a normal and customary way to establish a relationship or reinforce a connection, show respect, and assert yourself as the important person that you are.

Give a big hello even if it's a doctor you see regularly. If you're in a wheelchair and unable to get up, reach out your hand and say, "Hello," "Hi," "Hey," or "Good to see you!" Ask the doctor, "How are you?" Offer a handshake, a hug—do whatever makes you comfortable. Show your doctor how pleased you are to see him or her.

Make sure to introduce family and friends to your doctor. Of course your support team is already primed on the The Rules, so they can then sit back and let you be in charge of you. Having your family and friends also stand up to greet the doctor shows respect and warms up the meeting; it also asserts their importance.

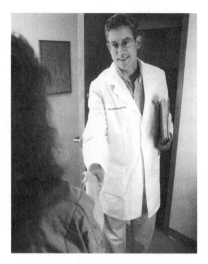

**Hello; hi; howdy, partner.**

## How Close? How Far?

I think that how far away you sit from your doctor can have an impact on your communication. Let's just say you've been diagnosed with a serious illness. From that first day you heard the diagnosis, fear took over, and you and your partner stopped having sex. You may have even tried to find solutions on your own.

**A girl's gotta do what a girl's gotta do.**

And you thought maybe, just maybe, other people might have had this problem, too. So, you thought you might ask your doctor for some real answers about reclaiming your sex life. But how can you get comfortable enough to ask these tough questions when the doctor is sitting so far away that you've got to shout things like, "How to I get my sex life back?"

Well, you can move your seat a little closer.

**That's better. Oh my, that's a very big mole.**

How close do you want to sit? Are you in your comfort zone?

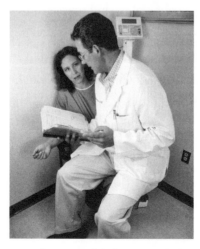

**Do you want to move close enough to have your doctor on your lap?**

You might find yourself in other settings where the distance inhibits your ability to share sensitive information. Sitting on the other side of a very big desk from your doctor is one such situation. To feel more comfortable, move your chair around the corner of the desk to get closer. If you feel funny doing this, just say that you're having a hard time hearing and you care very much about what he or she has to say. Using a sincere compliment can ease any uncomfortable feelings.

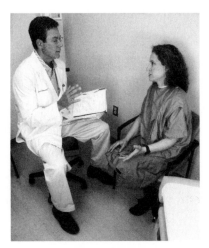

**This feels just right.**

## Express Yourself

At the beginning of your meeting, let your doctor know what's on your mind, even if you've already mentioned those concerns to the nurse. Explain how the doctor can be most helpful to you on that particular day. Bring your completed homework: a prepared list of questions and a report of your symptoms and concerns. (See the Symptom Reporting Sheet on page 27.) Put your most pressing questions at the top of the list. Organize the rest of the questions into mid- and low-level importance.

Make sure your list is typed or printed neatly on one sheet of paper, using large-size print so you can read your own questions quickly and easily. Don't write on the back of your hand or on a teeny-tiny piece of paper that will get lost at the bottom of your pocketbook. If you can't find your questions or you can't read what you've written, you won't get your questions answered. That would be a bummer, since getting some meaty answers was one of the big reasons why you went to see your doctor in the first place.

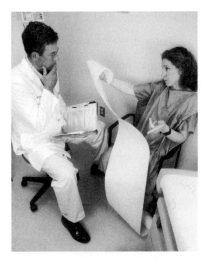

**Impressed? I did this all by myself.**

Your meeting with your doctor is more important than nearly any class you've prepared for in the past. So be sure to do all of this homework well before your visit. All of that homework training over the years was meant to help you prepare for the opportunities and challenges in your life. The only way to get the answers you're looking for is by asking well-thought-out questions. Just like you did in school, research your topic. Think about the larger picture, and then write down your questions, concerns, and symptoms.

Sometimes, when we're nervous after asking a question, we do the worst possible thing: we keep talking. To get the most information after you ask a question, it's critical to stop and listen to the answer. Give the doctor a chance to respond. Keep in mind that this is a relationship between two people. So, if you ask the doctor for information and you don't give him or her a chance to respond, the relationship could get strained. Your doctor doesn't feel heard, and the time and effort he or she is making to provide answers are wasted. The doctor might react, get exasperated, and may even get up to leave.

## Reasons for Poor Listening at the Doctor's Office

- **Being nervous**

- **Feeling pressured to share questions and concerns quickly, fearing that time will run out**

- **Not understanding the answer to a question**

- **Rushing the doctor so you can get a chance to ask the more useful questions**

- **Asking others' questions, which aren't of great interest to you**

- **Being afraid of what the doctor might tell you**

- **Focusing on asking the next question instead of on the answer to the one you just asked**

- **Losing your place in the conversation—and pretending to be back on top of things. Anxiety builds because you're still lost.**

- **Modifying additional questions in light of the answers you just received**

After asking each question, shift to listening mode and throw in some eye contact. Each time you get an answer that's helpful to you, acknowledge and thank your doctor. You could say something like, "Thank you. This information is really helpful to me." Or, "I really appreciate your answer. You're the first one who explained the information in a way that I can really understand." Showing your gratitude and reinforcing your doctor's special value to you makes a huge difference in your patient-doctor relationship. I guarantee that you will hear many more answers to the questions on your list.

### But My Doctor Doesn't Listen to Me!

You might be burning up right now, angry with me for urging you to listen to the doctor if your doctor rarely listens to you. I understand and share your frustration. You are right: Your doctor should do a better job of listening to you. However, when you are seeking your doctor's answers and advice, you need to be an expert listener. Tips on getting your doctor to listen to you can be found throughout the book.

As your seven minutes tick away, the time left for the rest of your questions quickly disappears. You didn't anticipate that it would take so long to tackle the first two questions on your list. Darn. Maybe you have too many questions on your list.

Maybe your questions were too general—not specific enough—and that's why your doctor answered with a long dissertation on the history of medicine that finally led up to the real take-home message you were seeking. Yes, a shorter answer would have sufficed—but you appreciated your doctor's interest and didn't want to interrupt. You went through a lot of preparation, juggling, and waiting to get to this moment. You've been disrobed, weighed, poked, and prodded. It's hard to think about the fact that you might have to wait again to get your other questions answered.

Before your doctor's up and at the door ready to leave, it's OK to say, "I know I have a lot of questions today and I can see that you're already running late. Can you help me make a plan to address the rest of my questions?" You can discuss whether it makes sense to schedule another appointment or a follow-up phone call. If the doctor works by e-mail, that may be a way to receive timely answers to your questions. Perhaps the doctor has other professionals on his or her team, such as nurses, physician's assistants, or physical therapists, who may be able to answer your questions. Or there may be other doctors who could be very helpful. Together, you can work out a plan to get the additional information that you need.

There are also some pitfalls in the question-and-answer part of your appointment that you should try to avoid. They can disrupt the use of your time, create tension between you and your doctor, and generally make your appointment less efficient. There are two uncomfortable question situations you should try to avoid:

## The "Quick Question"

When the doctor is about to leave the room, it is not the time to say, "Oh, Doctor, I have one more quick question." The so-called quick question is rarely that. More likely, it's your biggest question, possibly even a bombshell, such as, "Doctor, if this treatment doesn't work, does that mean I'm going to die?"

It's not uncommon for patients to leave the scariest question for the last possible moment, when the chance of getting an answer runs away. This may frustrate your doctor, leaving him or her to wonder why you spent the time allotted for the appointment discussing less urgent questions. Of course, human nature is not so rational when the information is scary and we're feeling threatened and vulnerable.

No apologies are necessary for this kind of thing. Still, you do need to be tuned into how you're thinking and feeling before you go to the doctor's office to achieve the best use of the time.

## Answers Without Credit

If you just asked a stack of questions, don't throw a bunch more out just as your doctor is about to leave the room, especially if you haven't acknowledged the answers that were already given. This implies that your doctor hasn't answered any of your questions during the very visit that is about to end.

Not giving your doctor credit—or maybe even extra credit—for all the answers he or she just gave you can suck the goodwill out of the relationship right at the moment when you are seeking more time, attention, and a good connection. But don't worry, this subtle issue is easily fixed or avoided by choosing the right words. Better to say, "Doctor, I am really grateful for the answers you've given to my many questions. I know you have to leave now and move on with your busy schedule—but I just realized that I have another question for you." Then quickly launch into your question. It may seem like a small point, but it can affect how you and your doctor relate to each other.

## What's with All of the Questions?

It may feel as if you're on a frenzied fact-finding mission when you're meeting with your doctor. But there are lots of reasons why you've got questions. It may be that answers to your initial questions lead to more questions, or that as you spoke to the doctor or other people you know, new concerns came up. The abundant health information on television and radio programs, as well as in magazines and newspapers and on the Internet, may raise questions about medical breakthroughs that you might not have heard of before. You may also feel as though the doctor hasn't answered your questions in a way that relieves your doubts.

It's fine to have questions. Asking a question is your way of getting your doctor to summarize the main messages so you can leave with a clear understanding of what's going on.

# ELEVEN

## The Capture

Grasping the Important Things Your Doctor Says

One of the toughest parts about being a patient is trying to absorb and retain everything your doctor says. Wait, forget *everything*—just getting all the main points is very difficult. Why is it so hard? Because listening, understanding, and remembering are nearly impossible to do when you are anxious and worried about your future. You're just not in the best state of mind to be dealing with all this complicated information.

So how do you capture this precious information?

One option is to take notes. Pay attention, listen and write, listen and write. The downside is that when you take your own notes, you lose most of your eye contact with the doctor. You may also miss your doctor's body language. This can disrupt your communication with the doctor.

What other options do you have? You can use a tape recorder. It's best to ask your doctor's permission to record his or her voice. In some states, legally capturing someone else's voice requires his or her consent. Your doctor might assume you are gathering evidence for a lawsuit. This is a relationship between two people.

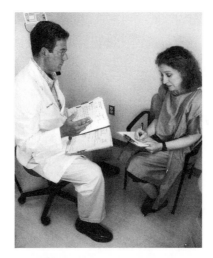

I have no idea what I am writing.

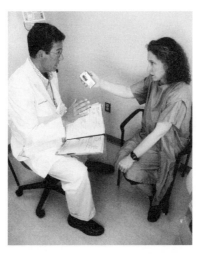

OK . . . go! Repeat after me: "I am your favorite patient."

You want a record of your medical discussion, and you also want your doctor to feel appreciated and respected. Here is one thing you can say: "I really value what you have to say. As soon as I get home, my whole family's going to ask me what happened at the doctor's office and I want to be able to tell them. So is it OK for me to record what you're saying?" Most doctors will agree to that request.

**Meet my friend Marcy. Mess with me and she'll land you sideways.**

Another option is to bring a friend and have him or her write down the information for you. Again, make sure you introduce this person to the doctor, while letting him or her know what can be said in front of your friend.

## Fading Away

When you're in the midst of the rapid-fire of complex medical information, you can feel overwhelmed, inadequate, and vulnerable. All it takes is a few sentences of medical mumbo jumbo—words that sound like a foreign language—to make you shrink, lose your place in the conversation, and start to fade away.

Sometimes, you feel yourself shrinking away and you start to feel like a child all over again.

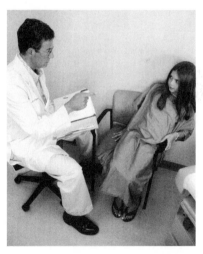

**Stay away from me. I want my mommy.**

Then, just as you are regaining your senses, starting to feel more in charge, the doctor might say something that makes you feel as if your life is passing you by. It's as if you've aged forty years in less than a minute.

All of sudden, you feel like your own mother.

**Everything aches. Do you have some hot tea with lemon?**

Fading in and out of the conversation is normal. It's nearly impossible to sustain a high level of attention for an extended period of time—especially when you're anxious, confused, and exhausted. When it's your life that's at stake, it becomes even more difficult. To keep the fading episodes short and be able to jump back into the conversation, begin by sitting up in your chair, taking a deep breath, and reasserting yourself.

Everyone wants to be heard. When you talk, you want your

doctor to listen. But there may come a time when you feel ignored. For example, what happens if your doctor is on the phone while he's talking to you?

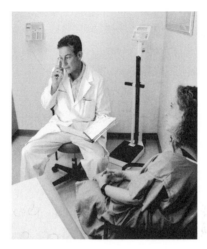

"No, really . . . tell me more!"

How can the doctor give you his full attention when he's on the phone? Before you lose your cool, think about who he might be talking to. Perhaps it's your surgeon calling your doctor with details about your case. This is exactly what you want to see happen. Let them talk without interruption. You might even take notes on what you can overhear of the conversation.

There may be other valid reasons for your doctor to interrupt your time together. He or she might be getting a call from another doctor about another patient's situation. It's best to let them talk. After all, you want to know that your doctor will grab the opportunity to catch another doctor about *your* situation— even if the timing isn't perfect and another patient is slightly inconvenienced. This kind of give-and-take always works in your favor, assuming that there is no violation of anyone's privacy by being present during these sensitive conversations.

On the other hand, what if it's the BMW car dealership calling about a problem with the doctor's car? Technically, while the slight rattle when the car turns left might limit your doctor's ability to get to and from work, your sympathy might also be limited. But a functional car is central to nearly everyone's life. My advice in this situation is to not object and to let it go, especially if the doctor apologizes after getting off the phone.

Now, if you're listening to your doctor talk to his buddy about football tickets, you have a right to feel upset and insulted. Depending on the length of the conversation and your mood, you may choose to let it go as long as this conversation doesn't take away from your seven or more minutes. Or you may express your frustration with body language or a polite but clear comment.

What do you do if the doctor wants to both carry on the phone conversation and also keep talking to you? If he or she is on the phone, you can say, "I'll just wait till you're off the phone so I can get your full attention." You might begin to do something else while he or she handles outside business. While you wait, write a list, organize your wallet or purse, or pull out your book.

If you're concerned that your doctor hasn't heard a thing you've just said, you might reconfirm the key points of your conversation. Tell your doctor that you know the two of you have discussed quite a bit, and that you very much want to hear the doctor's response to your question or feedback on your concerns. This may give the doctor a chance to refocus. You may need to repeat your questions or concerns, but it's a gentle way to remind the doctor that you need proper attention.

The reality is that just like you, the doctor has been working hard all day and might fade here or there. He or she is only human and might need a way to sneak back into the conversation without losing face. Don't scold your doctor if this happens. That may just create tension for the little remaining time that you have.

While there is no excuse for poor listening, it's just not something that you are going to fix when you are in the process of getting medical care. We all have imperfections. Keep in mind that your whole purpose for being at the appointment is to get what you want and need from your doctor visit and your relationship with your doctor. If being flexible and forgiving helps you rescue the discussion with your doctor, your personal effort will likely pay off. When the conversation gets back to a more comfortable place and the communication is flowing, you both win.

There is no question that the relationship with your doctor can be complicated and hard to navigate. During your doctor visit—under all the pressure, strain, and suspense—strange things can happen.

In fact, there is something else that can happen that we rarely discuss because it is oh-so-taboo. It's what our minds might do—on their own, without our consent—to release the strain of built-up pressure. And that's fantasy. It's not just fantasy that your doctor will make you well. I can tell you from personal experience that your mind will drift. It will wander. And it only takes a millisecond to imagine what your doctor might look like without clothes.

**Oh, no. It's really not my fault. Innocent by virtue of insanity
in a moment of intense fear.**

We can only hope that your mind will come back quickly. When it does return, you may have missed everything the doctor just said. If so, say something like, "I'm sorry but I think I missed the last point you made. Do you remind repeating it please?" Then, go on from there.

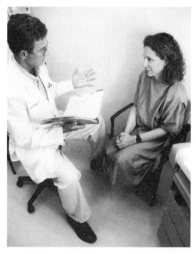

**OK, I'm back again. Sometimes reality is better than fantasy.**

# TWELVE

## Passing the Physical Exam

Coming to After Full Exposure

**Y**ou've had a chance to talk. Now, it's time for the physical exam. Before it starts, I like to see my doctor wash his or her hands before touching me.

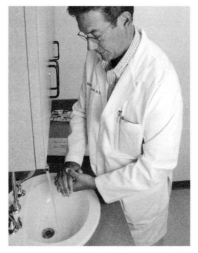

**Good idea: soap and warm water. I'm liking you more and more.**

Washing hands helps to avoid spreading germs from one patient to another. That is why it is so important for your doctor to wash his or her hands between patients. Your doctor may have washed his or her hands before entering your room. In that situation, he or she might say, "I just washed my hands before coming in, so I'll proceed to your physical exam." That's fine. If you suspect that's not the case, particularly if you notice that your doctor is constantly stroking his mustache or beard, or rubbing his or her nose or ears during the meeting leading up to your exam, you may need to drop a hint or two.

## How to Get Your Doctor to Wash His or Her Hands

1.  "You always wash your hands before the physical exam and I really appreciate that."

2.  "Wow—you really have a nice-looking soap dispenser there."

3.  "What makes a soap antibacterial, Dr. Smith? Is it really better than regular soap?"

4.  "I'm amazed doctors don't get sick more often. It must be because they always wash their hands before touching their patients, right?"

5.  "What is that gunk under your fingernails?"

My own house is a messy place with three kids, two dogs, and my husband and his fishing obsession. Add them up and they equal chaos. However, it's necessary for my whole medical office environment to feel therapeutic: clean, orderly, professional. My white coat and my team members' uniforms are clean. Hands and fingernails are washed. The discussion and examination rooms are scrubbed. The place where we take care of patients has to be hygienic and show that we take our profession very seriously. Not that it's easy—we're constantly on the lookout for dirty corners, dusty light fixtures, or empty soap dispensers and paper towel racks. When we find them, we correct them. By keeping the office neat and clean, we provide the best possible health care environment for our patients.

*OK. Now it is time for the physical exam.*

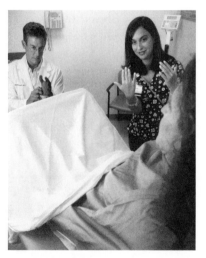

**A little more . . . no . . . further still . . . whoa . . . you've gone too far. Back 'er up!**

Personally, I have always been embarrassed by the gynecologic examination. And I know from loads of research and chit-chats with my friends that I'm not the only one who feels this way. In fact, it turns out that women's dread of the gynecologic exam is a common reason why many women don't see their gynecologists on a regular basis.

What I can share with you is a little solution that I came up with while I was giving birth to twins in a room filled with thirty doctors and nurses (my husband and I were both doctors working at that hospital, so they made sure that all doctors were present and every base was covered). It's sort of a secret.

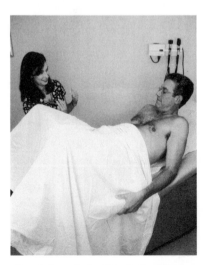

**Scoot down just a little further, Hank.**

To get over my discomfort, I just imagine the doctor in those stirrups. Yes, it's a bit silly, but if it helps me get over my embarrassment, who cares?

The physical exam is very important. Be sure to point out anything that you've felt or seen that you're concerned about. But it's best to hold your other questions and comments until after the physical so your doctor can concentrate on doing a careful exam.

So far, there has been a chance to talk. I've asked all my questions, and the doctor gave me his answers. I had the physical exam, which wasn't *so* bad. Now it's time to pull everything together. I look up and see his face.

**Keep biting your tongue—I don't want the bad news.**

Oh NO! OH GOD! He looks so serious. I immediately imagine the worst. Something must be terribly wrong. Clearly, he's struggling to find the right words to deliver the bad news. That's it. I'm dead. I'm buried. There's my husband with another woman!

I can't believe it. He's lusting for her!

And then there's that tramp baking another cake and celebrating my kid's birthday!

**OK, it looks as if she can bake, but I bet she can't cook.**

Finally, I refocus, and I start to hear what my doctor's saying.

**He's smiling? He's smiling!**

He's telling me that everything's OK. I feel so much better. He's done *his* homework—read all my records, seen my films, talked to my other doctors, and examined me. Having him so involved in my life and on top of my medical situation all feels so reassuring. I can feel that he cares and that he's there for me. I can see that he's pleased to have me as one of his patients. From everything he's saying and doing, I feel that my health care is in good hands. He stands ready to be my advocate.

That's really the best part of the doctor-patient relationship— that intimate, private, intense exchange between two people about something that couldn't be more serious and sacred: your life and your health. Even if the news isn't good, as long as your doctor explains everything to you, provides a plan of action, and makes it clear that he or she cares about you and is available when you need him or her, you can regain a sense of control over your situation. It's tremendously reassuring.

# THIRTEEN

## Following Up

Getting Tests Reported, Questions Answered,
Prescriptions Refilled, and Calls Returned

Excellent care requires excellent communication, not just between you and your doctor, but among all the doctors on your team. Your doctor should pick up the phone and call your other doctors, when necessary, to make sure that everyone's on the same page. If your doctor writes or dictates a letter to summarize the findings of your visit, you want to make sure that it's sent to the other physicians on your team. If a test is ordered, check that other doctors' names are on that slip, marked as "cc," which stands for carbon copy. That way, everyone gets a copy of the report.

If you haven't already done so, make a list of your doctors' names, addresses, phone numbers, and e-mail addresses. It's a good idea to do the same thing for your spouse and your children. That way, when the time comes to send off the reports, you won't have the additional aggravation of hunting for contact info. Be sure that you provide this contact information to each person on your entire medical team.

You can help by typing up a list of all the doctors to whom you want copies sent, along with their addresses and phone and fax numbers. Put your primary doctors on top of the list. If you leave your doctor's office with your slip and there are no other doctors' names on the test request, then it's perfectly fine to write your other doctors' names on there yourself. Remember, you are the boss of your medical records, including selecting who can—and who can't—get access to your medical information, including test results, diagnoses, and the like.

Later, when you get the test done, be sure to inform the testing center about who needs to get reports—even if it's already plainly written on the slip. Hand the receptionist the same list of doctors with their contact information to make it easier for the center to send out reports. Don't be surprised if they will only send reports to two or, possibly, three doctors. With hospital cutbacks, two-report limits are becoming more common. Unfortunately, a lot of people don't know about this limitation. They give their slip or list to the testing center loaded with doctors' names. Only much later do they find out that only two reports were sent, leaving the rest of their doctors in the dark.

So that you're clear about their policies, ask if the testing center will send out additional reports and if there is an extra fee. Make yourself a recipient of one of those copies. Then, you can make as many copies as you need to send out to the rest of your doctors.

Dealing with seemingly random policies like this can be frustrating. But don't let this kind of frustration with the medical system sour your relationship with your doctor. Letting your doctor know about these kinds of issues is fine if you think it's really necessary. If you choose to do so, make it clear that you're not blaming him or her *personally* for the problem. Making your doctor feel defensive about something over which he or she has no control can sink a ship. But your doctor does want to know when you hit snags in the system, so he or she can fix them, go around them, or better prepare you, or the next patient, for them.

If you believe you have suffered harm as a result of your doctor's treatment, let that doctor know. Find out why things went wrong and give him or her the chance to be accountable. If your doctor has neglected to convey urgent medical information, you are well within your rights to complain. However, if you are depressed, angry, overwhelmed, and fearful about your *health*—all of which can be normal reactions to a serious medical crisis—yet you are satisfied with the *care* you are receiving, don't thrust all your anger, frustration, and anxiety on your doctor. That can be poisonous. Your relationship with your doctor is precious and delicate, so proceed with caution.

Do, however, communicate those feelings to your doctor without blame. By saying something like, "I'm feeling overwhelmed by anger, frustration, and anxiety due to my health. Your help getting me through and beyond this health challenge is greatly appreciated. What are my next best steps in dealing with both the emotional and physical issues I'm up against?"

What happens when you have questions or a request after you leave the doctor's office? You call and you speak to the doctor's secretary, receptionist, administrative assistant, or nurse.

Establishing a good relationship with the doctor's office personnel can make everything go more smoothly. It can help you with getting a convenient appointment; having your doctor return your phone call in a timely manner; granting referrals to other doctors and approvals on tests ordered; getting paperwork filled out for work, disability, and other benefits; getting prescriptions called in; and more.

When you call the doctor's office, immediately find out the name of the person to whom you are speaking. Greet the person by name and then politely find out his or her position in the department. Ask—don't guess—the person's role. Some people can get very sensitive about their rank in the doctor's office. You might say, "Jane, I'd appreciate your helping me as I try to get to know how Dr. Jones's office works. Can you tell me what your role is on the team?" Then, thank her for the information. Knowing each person's name and role helps you know to whom you should direct your request, or question about an issue that might come up in the future.

Next, let the person answering the phone know exactly why you are calling. Give as much information as you can. It's a good idea to only say it's private if, in fact, it's really private. The more specific you are, the better able your doctor will be to respond to your request. If your doctor is running around all day long and is rarely at his or her desk, where most messages are left, by the time he or she returns to finds your message with no details, he or she might not have time to track down the information you need. Alternatively, if you provide a detailed message early in the day, the doctor's staff can often find the information that you're seeking, such as a pathology report, a blood test, a culture result, and the like, and attach it to your message. That way, the doctor can easily call you with the information you need. It's also possible that someone other than the doctor can help. For example, if you're calling about a prescription refill, then the staff can usually get your doctor's approval and call in the refill during the day. Then, it's ready for you to pick up long before the doctor might have even called back.

Here are two reasons why you might be calling, along with a list of specific details to include in your message:

## The Prescription Refill

- **Name of the medicine**

- **Dose of the medicine (it should be written on the bottle's label)**

- **Frequency that you take the medicine**

- **How long you've been taking it**

- **Any medication allergies**

- **Details of the pharmacy where you want the prescription filled, including name, specific branch, telephone number, and hours of operation**

- **The doctor who originally prescribed the medication**

NOTE: Keep all your medical contact information on one piece of paper, including the phone number of your pharmacy and the name of the pharmacist, if possible.

## Getting Test Results

- **The test about which you're calling**

- **The location where the test was done**

- **The date the test was done**

- **The doctor who requested the test**

- **The best method for the doctor to reach you with the results, with all phone numbers where you can be reached for the next twenty-four hours from the time of your call**

- **The times that the doctor can call you with the results**

- **If you're not available, whether the doctor can leave the results on your answering machine or whether the doctor has permission to leave the information with anyone else. If so, be clear about whom.**

Communication beyond the doctor's office can sometimes occur by letter. This can work extremely well, as you have a document in hand that spells out the results of a test or an opinion on a question. That is, it's helpful if you understand the letter and if the report is complete. However, letters can fail if the words read like a foreign language and no one is there to help you understand the terminology.

Here's an example of a real letter one of my patients received that shows how this can backfire:

*Dear Mrs. Smith,*

*I tried calling you both at home and at work and was unable to reach you. I want to advise you that the CT scan showed no evidence of cancer—just aseptic necrosis.*

*Sincerely,*

*Dr. Jones*

This patient had no idea what "aseptic necrosis" was. She got the letter on a Friday and was terribly worried all weekend long. On Monday, she called the doctor's office but his assistant said that he was on vacation. When she called me on Monday afternoon, she was a wreck. Only then did she find out what aseptic necrosis meant: poor blood supply, which leads to breakdown of the bone. While she still had a significant medical problem, I was able to explain to her that it was manageable and not life-threatening. Knowing was much better than not knowing and worrying.

# FOURTEEN

## Second Opinions

It's My Right . . . Right?

**A** second opinion is the opportunity for you to get more information so that you can make the best decisions possible. It doesn't mean that you're being disloyal to your doctors or disrespectful of their authority, knowledge, or experience.

While it's natural to feel awkward and uncomfortable, operate from a position of strength and don't be defensive. After all, you're doing a vital job: you're taking care of the one and only you.

It's fine to let your current doctors know that you're seeking a second opinion to get more perspective, more information, or confirmation, or so that you can feel more resolved and ready to move forward under the doctor's care. Your relationship with your doctor is not a binding commitment like marriage, and getting a second opinion is not like having an affair. If telling your doctor that you want a second opinion makes you feel uncomfortable, simply say that your family insists on it.

Every time you seek another medical consultation, however, you may leave with another opinion and a different set of recommendations. There are many reasons why opinions can differ:

**There may be more than one "right" answer.** There may be many ways to manage one particular situation. In fact, it's likely that you might come up with more than one viable option for your care.

**New information may emerge.** As time goes by, new doctors can take advantage of additional testing and treatment information to help shape and refine their recommendations. They may seem smarter than your first doctor—but it might just mean that the new information made them seem smarter.

**Doctors have different styles.** Some doctors tend to be more medically aggressive, adopting a more-is-better, go-for-broke attitude with testing and treatment recommendations. Others may be more laid-back and feel that less is more when it comes to medical procedures or medication. In certain places, like New York City, doctors tend to follow more aggressive treatment options because patients want to be more proactive in their care. How you present yourself to one doctor compared to another can bring out this tendency. For example, if you say "I want to do everything possible" to one doctor and you say "I want to do everything reasonable" to another doctor, you might receive different recommendations.

**Different geographic areas have different institutional and regional traditions.** You might live in an area with a dominant medical culture, like Cleveland, where the Cleveland Clinic's approach to heart disease tends to rule the area. In New York, Memorial Sloan-Kettering Cancer Center has a profound effect on how New Yorkers are treated for cancer. In California, complementary medicine shares front-row seating with conventional medicine, whereas in Florida, conventional medicine dominates. The area in which you're receiving your opinion may cause it to vary.

**Generational differences can affect opinions.** Some doctors tend to give aggressive treatment recommendations to younger patients and less aggressive advice to older patients. You might come across as young to one doctor and older to another, depending on the age of the doctor and how you appear and present yourself.

**Doctors might favor their own specialties.** Most doctors feel most comfortable and most confident in their own area of expertise. As a result, opinions and recommendations from different doctors within different specialties might lean toward their own field—yet still be objective and correct. For example, a surgeon might favor back surgery for a painful slipped disc and a neurologist might recommend pain medication and physical therapy.

**Personal constraints may affect opinions.** Outside forces can also affect testing and treatment recommendations, such as financial debt, restricted medical insurance coverage, medication cost issues, limited resources available where you live, or practical daily constraints on your life from work, home, family, and community demands.

For your own sake, it's always helpful to know why you're seeking a second opinion. Knowing your reasons for a second opinion will help you fulfill your expectations.

## Common Reasons for a Second Opinion

**Package Deal.** You want your whole situation checked out by a new team of doctors from all specialties that pertain to your situation. For example, if you have a diagnosis of cancer, you want to know if chemotherapy is necessary in your situation. You also know that getting a second opinion at a university hospital usually involves a complete reevaluation, from pathology review of the tissue (aka "slide review") to a second radiologist's review of your X-rays, MRI scans, and so forth. Or, if you have a heart problem, you might want to see another heart duo, which includes a cardiologist and a heart surgeon, also called a cardiothoracic surgeon.

**Balanced Perspective.** Let's say you have heart disease and you're trying to make a decision between continued medical management, the placement of a stent to hold open a blocked artery, or a major open-heart bypass procedure. Perhaps you've already received an aggressive approach to treatment: a heart surgeon told you that you absolutely must have bypass surgery, saying, "If you were my wife, mother, or sister, you would have already had it." His or her recommendations might be absolutely correct—but you're feeling overwhelmed and scared. You may want another opinion from a cardiologist who specializes in medicine therapies as well as stent procedures and who tends to be less surgically aggressive.

**Confirmation.** While you already have an opinion with which you're comfortable, you wish to check out the proposed plan of treatment with another expert before you proceed.

**Family Demands.** Even if you are perfectly happy with your current team of doctors and ready to get started on the proposed treatment plan, perhaps your family isn't so sure. They just won't leave you alone until you get a second opinion. While you want to get it over with quickly, since you're feeling pushed to do it, you realize that you might as well learn as much as possible from the additional evaluation.

**Insurance Company Requirements.** Perhaps the proposed treatment option is serious or risky, such as back surgery, hip replacement, or coronary artery bypass. Your insurance company may want confirmation from another doctor who also believes it's medically necessary. Or, you may be exploring a treatment option that is more expensive than the usual standard of care for your medical insurance plan, such as a special tissue transfer technique for reconstruction after mastectomy as opposed to a more traditional implant or belly-muscle flap. Before it agrees to pay for the procedure, your insurance carrier may require another expert opinion to prove that the procedure or treatment is reasonable and necessary.

**Tiebreaker.** Maybe you've already had two opinions, and each one gave a completely different recommendation of treatment. You're feeling confused, frustrated, and maybe even desperate. Getting a third opinion on whether Opinion A or Opinion B is the best course of action might settle the decision. To best manage expectations and to come out of the visit feeling more resolved, it's best to be upfront with the tiebreaker doctor. Explain that you've already received two opinions with different recommendations and that you're unsure about how to proceed. Don't be afraid if the doctor's expert opinion turns out to be something completely different—an Opinion C. If in fact you get a third option, it might be your best choice.

Intermittent Consultation. Having another physician act as a consultant can provide you with additional advice and insight both at the beginning of and throughout your treatment plan. Having someone other than your primary treating physician can give you a fresh perspective on an issue or help you find out about clinical trials or experimental therapies elsewhere. For example, I take care of a number of women with metastatic breast cancer who require continuous treatment in order to keep the cancer under control. All along the way, they are trying to figure out what the next best treatment option might be just in case the current therapy stops working. The arrangement between the treating physician and the consultant (me) works well because both doctors provide indispensable roles that are complementary. Their local cancer doctor still feels that he or she is in charge of providing the direct care—and is not threatened by the consultant doctor's intermittent expert input. Some of these patients are able to participate in a clinical trial offered at the consultant's institution but administered at the local treatment center. (This kind of collaboration isn't automatic—you have to choose doctors who enjoy this type of collegial relationship.)

## When the Doctor-Patient Relationship Breaks Down

Doctor-patient relationships are like other kinds of relationships. Sometimes they just don't work anymore. You may feel as if your doctor is arrogant and doesn't really care about you. Perhaps he or she doesn't take you seriously. Your relationship with your doctor may have unraveled and the fear of being stranded without a doctor has you in a panic to find someone new. The good news is that your experience has probably given you a better idea of what you're looking for in a new doctor. But how do you go about finding a new physician?

Getting a second—or even a third—opinion on a medical condition can be a good way to find someone with whom you're more compatible. As you go from doctor to doctor to find the one whom you like and trust the most, be sure to check out their staffs, facilities, and parking, as well as the convenience of their treatment protocol, treatment style, and location. If you're looking for a personality fit, try to find a doctor who reflects the characteristics that matter most to you. You may wish to see someone who is your own gender, age, or ethnic group or who speaks the same language that you do. If you are a mother, would you relate best to a doctor who is also a mother and who might be more likely to share similar concerns and values? Or you may be looking for someone who will just tell you what to do and stop forcing you to make the decisions. There are many patients—particularly from the older generations—who feel uncomfortable making complex decisions on unfamiliar issues. They are much more comfortable with the old-fashioned approach, in which doctors told patients what to do.

# FIFTEEN

## Changing Doctors

Can I Get Arrested for This?

f you've already decided to change doctors, it's best to establish a new relationship with the next doctor before you say good-bye to your old one. Save your precious personal energy and invest it in your relationship with your new doctor. Avoid the enormous energy cost of giving the old doctor a piece of your mind when you are full of frustration, hurt, and anger. You might feel better in the moment, but it may leave you exhausted and depleted for days, which is not a good strategy for moving forward. There may be an opportunity later, when you are settled into your relationship with your new doctor and everything is dandy, to tell the first doctor why you made that choice. Informing this doctor by letter is usually most effective, controllable, and comfortable.

As you consider new doctors, it's best to have a good idea of what you're looking for and why your relationship with your last doctor didn't work out. Have you even thought about this before? Do you spend more time shopping for the perfect TV than you do selecting a doctor?

**Tell me you love me!**

## Qualities to Look for in a Doctor

**Good Training.** Your doctor should be trained by a respected institution, and by recognized expert teachers and mentors.

**Experience.** It's usually best if your doctor has worked in the field for at least several years and has developed decision-making skills that are improved by experience.

**Thoroughness.** Your doctor should give careful attention to detail without rushing through a complete evaluation.

**Supportiveness.** Your doctor should put your interests first above all other competing interests, including making referrals that are not influenced by political ties to their own hospital network; resisting pressures to limit critical tests and additional medical opinions; and resolving possible conflicts with the doctor's office staff. You also want your doctor to go out of his or her way when appropriate—even if very inconvenient. It means so much when your doctor is willing to stay late to help you handle an urgent matter or to interrupt his or her precious personal time to help you through a tough situation. You want a doctor who knows when not to recommend a procedure, even though he or she may get paid to perform it.

**Confidence and Decisiveness.** Your doctor should help you make decisions and feel good about them. Avoid a doctor who waffles back and forth for an extended period of time, making you feel insecure.

**Good Listening Skills.** It's so important to have a doctor who actively listens to your questions and thoughtfully considers your concerns. Your doctor should take the time to answer your most important questions, follow up with lingering concerns, and direct unanswered questions—as appropriate—to other doctors or health care professionals with more expertise on the topics in question.

**Openness to Input.** The best doctors have respect for your own opinions about your symptoms, treatment, and options without being dismissive, arrogant, or condescending.

**Familiarity.** Your doctor should show some knowledge of your situation after you've been there a couple of times. Thoughtful doctors ask about your family and get to know key aspects about your home life. It's also reassuring when your doctor shows respect for your significant other, regardless of your sexual preference or personal living arrangement.

**Accessibility.** You should be able to reach your doctor when you need him or her. Calls should be returned within a reasonable time frame.

**Compassion.** Your doctor should understand that health questions can be confusing and frightening and respond with patience and kindness. Your doctor should establish eye contact, speak clearly, and repeat information patiently when asked. Your doctor should talk to you, not at you.

**Respect for Privacy.** Your doctor should never discuss your health or personal information in front of other people, even your support team, without your clear consent.

**Respect for Boundaries.** Together, you and your doctor should set limits that work for your relationship. Your doctor politely inquires about your family, but doesn't intrude in your personal life in a way that makes you uncomfortable. Your doctor is compassionate but not paternalistic or patronizing. Your doctor prescribes medications that you can afford. He or she gives you an exercise plan that is realistic for you to fulfill, and recommends a diet that is practical and healthy but not punitive. To make sure that your boundaries are respected, let your doctor know up front what works best for you.

This also applies to appropriate physical contact, which might be a solid handshake for some, a pat on the back for others, or even a hug. Personal preferences vary quite a bit. Such contact shows that your doctor cares about you, respects your cultural beliefs and values your relationship. However, you should make clear what type of contact is most comfortable for you.

**Appropriate Use of Humor.** Your doctor should crack jokes at the right time—and stay away from sensitive topics, religious or moral issues, and politics.

As you consider your needs, you should also consider the career stage of your doctor, considering whether this is a person with whom you can build a sustainable relationship. For example, if you have a long-term medical condition like high blood pressure, inflammatory bowel disease, diabetes, or cancer, you will want your doctor to be there for you over an extended period of time. Don't go to a doctor who is about to retire, unless he or she is a top expert in the field or region and his or her role is limited and well-defined, such as to give a second opinion or perform a highly specialized surgical procedure. Otherwise, you'll be putting effort into a relationship that will soon end, leaving you with the task of finding yet another doctor.

Gender can also be an issue in choosing a new doctor. Some people only feel comfortable with a doctor of the same gender, some prefer the opposite. Know your comfort zone. If you are from a country where most gynecologists are women, like China, and that's what you'd prefer, then find a female gynecologist. If you can't imagine having a woman urologist examine your penis and testicles, then find a male urologist. But try not to be too rigid on the gender issue. If the best doctor in town is a different gender from the one that you prefer, it's usually best to opt for the best medical care. Try hard to make it work.

There are other factors to consider in the package deal as you select a doctor:

Staff. Your doctor's secretaries, nurses, and other staff should be caring and responsive. Instead of blocking your access to your doctor, they should answer appropriate questions and arrange the time to talk to your doctor for answers that they can't address. They should help you get an appointment when you need it.

Admitting Privileges. Doctors must have privileges to work in a particular hospital. Ask about the hospitals in which your doctor is authorized to practice, perform surgery, or handle emergencies. This might make a big difference if you have a heart condition, and you are choosing a cardiologist. With your selection of a cardiologist comes a package deal of other doctors and services. You want to know the package deal up front. Or maybe you have active asthma and the ambulance, by regulation, always takes you to the nearest emergency room (ER). In that case, choose a doctor who has a working relationship with that ER.

Facilities. Look for a doctor's office that is housed in a well-lit, secure building that seems professionally managed and maintained. It should be in a central location with sufficient parking. Close to home, work, or shopping, depending on your needs. The office should be clean and pleasant, with adequate seating, reading material, and other amenities, such as a watercooler or toys and books for young children.

Beyond the characteristics of the office, there is one more essential ingredient that can make the biggest single difference and trumps all of the criteria listed above. That's finding a doctor who loves being a doctor. A passionate doctor thrives on taking care of people. He or she is going to be excited and empowered by new medical advances in his or her field of expertise, not threatened by them. A doctor who really loves the profession is more likely to go out of his or her way to talk to you, examine you, answer questions, solve problems, and stay in touch with your other doctors.

Another benefit of having a doctor who loves what she or he does is having a much better team. The doctor is the leader of the team, and his or her coworkers and employees pick up cues, energy, compassion, spirit, and a sense of professionalism from the doctor.

There's only one of you out there in the world, with your own set of needs, wants, preferences, and priorities. When selecting a doctor and approaching your overall care, remember who you are and what's most important to you, then work to honor yourself and respect your relationship with your doctors.

# SIXTEEN

## It Goes Both Ways

Making a Good Relationship Great

hen you do find a doctor with the **necessary knowledge, expertise, and judgment whom you really like—who also can relate to you,** care about you, listen, and is accessible to you and who enjoys taking care of you—wow! How therapeutic! Feeling as if you're in good care is the magic that fulfills the sacred covenant that you have with your doctor: to protect and cherish your life.

Whenever I am lucky enough to create a successful relationship with my doctor, I find ways to say thank you, again and again, to my doctor and his or her team.

**A thousand times—thank you!**

Those two simple words—thank you—mean so much to both doctors and their teams. Saying thank you is an acknowledgment that medicine and healing often go beyond charts and prescriptions and that doctors often go beyond the call of duty.

You can thank your medical team in person or with a simple note. If your doctor has really outdone him- or herself, it might be appropriate to give a gift such as a plant or food, or even tchotchkes, such as a candle, or a scarf or tie. All of these thankyous work well at different times for different people.

Now that I've taken you through my experience as a patient, it's time to get back into my role as a doctor.

**Great, I can finally warm up a bit.**

**"Marisa," "Hey you," "Dr. Weiss"—call me whatever you like.**

I feel very privileged to be asked to protect and cherish other people's lives. I thank my patients for that honor, usually saying, "Thank you so much for the privilege and pleasure of taking care of you."

There is only one of you and your life is precious. Medicine is a sacred profession. Your doctors are given the honor and responsibility to help you protect and cherish your life to the best of their ability. When you take an active role in your care, you demonstrate one of the highest forms of self-respect and empowerment. By informing your doctor of who you are, how you prefer to receive your care, and your style of making decisions, you are helping her or him do a much better job of taking care of you.

I want to share a story about one of my patients who was diagnosed with prostate cancer. At the time, I was taking care of women with breast cancer and men with prostate cancer. During his seven-week course of treatment, I tried hard to get to know him.

"How was your weekend?" I would ask.

"OK," he replied.

"Did you get stuffed on Thanksgiving?" I would ask with a cheerful smile.

"Yes," was his monosyllabic reply.

"What team are you rooting for in the Super Bowl?"

"Eagles," he said.

He was a man of very few words and I found that a challenge to deal with. What was he thinking? What was he feeling? I couldn't help but look for a connection between his limited words and his satisfaction with his medical care. Finally, at the end of his treatment, it was time for me to get a few words in, whether he liked it or not.

"Thank you, Mr. Johnson, for the privilege of being your doctor," I said warmly, studying his face intently.

I reached forward to offer him a hug. He froze a bit but must have known it was coming since he had seen me hug other patients who had finished their treatment. With the release of my embrace, Mr. Johnson quickly said good-bye and scurried out of the clinic. I went into another room with the next patient, feeling a little disheartened that I hadn't managed to crack through his reserved demeanor. Despite knowing that I had given him the best care possible, his lack of responsiveness shook my confidence.

As I tried to shift my focus to the patient sitting in front of me, all of a sudden, I could hear music coming down the hallway. What was going on?

I opened the door and there was Mr. Johnson.

**How do I look?**

He had gone out to his car, put on his Mummers costume, donned his accordion, and returned to the office to say thank you to me and my team. What a truly wonderful gift for all of us! And what a lesson for me: Every patient I see is truly a unique individual. Everyone has his or her own history, family, loves, fears, beliefs, values, and ways of expressing him- or herself. When both doctor and patient are dedicated to giving and getting the best care possible, any two styles of communication can be bridged by their sacred relationship; a relationship founded on care, compassion, trust, respect, and science. Whether I'm wearing the white jacket or the blue gown, I keep that lesson in mind.

# Conclusion

Your life is your greatest gift, and it's your responsibility to protect and cherish it through the best health care possible. With today's life expectancy being longer than it's ever been, more years of precious life are at stake. But you don't have to shoulder the responsibility of your health on your own. Your doctor is there to help.

Gone are the days of leisurely doctor visits, house calls, one all-knowing doctor, and the obedient patient. You can and must take an active role in your care in order to achieve the best health possible—even if you only get seven minutes with your doctor.

Whether you are going for a routine checkup or for a serious medical procedure, take charge. Think of yourself as a partner with your doctor in your care. Use this book's ready-to-use tips to prepare for your visit; stay focused, calm, and in control during the visit; and know what to do in the follow-up period. Everyone in the doctor's office, from receptionist to nurse to doctor, is there because of you and for you.

Remember: There is only one of *you*. Do not sink to feeling nameless and faceless, like "Diabetic Number Forty-five" or "Cancer Patient Number One Hundred." Don't let the multiple treatment options overwhelm you. Don't be intimidated by the inherently lopsided relationship between patient and doctor. The playing field has leveled a few degrees. Patients have greater power and a stronger voice.

You deserve the best. Even a little extra effort can improve the relationship you have with your doctor. A bigger effort can produce an even stronger bond. Just knowing that there is someone to call, someone on whom you can depend, someone to help you find the best possible care in a time of need is powerful medicine.

Getting the best care possible will make it more likely for you to lead a comfortable, joyful, exciting, and meaningful life—on your own and within your family, work and community arenas. With this book and best wishes—I hope that you will enjoy the best of health today and well into your future!

## Personal Medical Information

Insurance _____

Group # _____

Individual # _____

Mailing address _____

_____

E-mail _____

## Notes

_____

_____

_____

_____

_____

_____

_____

_____

_____

_____

_____

_____

## Doctors

Name _____

Specialty _____

Address _____

_____

Phone number _____

E-mail _____


Name _____

Specialty _____

Address _____

_____

Phone number _____

E-mail _____


Name _____

Specialty _____

Address _____

_____

Phone number _____

E-mail _____

## Doctors

Name _____

Specialty _____

Address _____

_____

Phone number _____

E-mail _____


Name _____

Specialty _____

Address _____

_____

Phone number _____

E-mail _____


Name _____

Specialty _____

Address _____

_____

Phone number _____

E-mail _____